Attitude Adjustment

Make Your Whole Outlook Brand New

Nancy N. Wilson

Published in the United States of America
First Edition September 2012

While all attempts have been made to verify information provided in this publication, the Publisher assumes no responsibility for errors, omissions, or contrary interpretation of the subject matter herein. Any perceived slights of specific persons, peoples, or organizations are unintentional.

This material is designed to provide general information about the subject matter covered. The author and publisher are not engaged in rendering legal, financial, medical, or psychological advice. If expert assistance is required in these areas, the services of a professional should be sought.

ASIN: B009638IUDQ (eBook)
ISBN: ISBN-13: 978-1479326136 (Paperback)

Published by Blurtigo Holdings, LLC
P. O. Box 1173
Gilbert, AZ 85299

Thank You

. . . for buying my book.
If you enjoy it, please review it on Amazon.com

For a complete list of my published books, please visit my Author's Page...

https://amazon.com/author/nancywilson

TABLE OF CONTENTS

Introduction

Attitude can be your most powerful tool in living a good life. Your attitude creates an aura that is positive or negative and becomes the magnet that draws people to you or pushes them away. What you project through your attitude is, in large part, the catalyst for the kinds of attitudes that you receive from others. If you are happy, positive, creative, optimistic, accepting, and loving . . .OR . . .if you are unhappy, negative, defeated, critical, pessimistic, sad, and angry – in most situations, the same attitude will be reflected back to you.

When the idea for this book came to me, I remembered a popular song from years ago, *Attitude Adjustment*, by Hank Williams, Jr. Of course, since it was a country western song written by a country western rebel, the manner in which the attitude adjustment was made is not what I recommend, but the final words are worth remembering, *"It made my whole outlook brand new."*

If your life is not what you want it to be in one or all aspects, the problem may be closely related to your attitude. That is the purpose of this book – to help you really look at your approach to life and the attitude you project.

Is your attitude serving you or hurting you? As you read through each section of the book, you will find information, exercises and suggestions to help you with attitude adjustments that can make your whole outlook brand new.

Part One

Is Your Attitude Your Friend or Your Enemy?

Your attitude can be your best friend – a friend that can help you build the kind of life you want that is filled with laughter and joy. Or, it can be your worst enemy – an enemy that defeats you at every turn and causes you to continually struggle with negativity and rejection.

Your attitude paints your life with hues and shades of happiness and contentment or with hues and shades of sadness and discontent. What colors fill the world in which you live?

Attitude reigns supreme and impacts every facet of your life. If you want to feel good, be happy and content, build solid relationships, and move forward successfully in your chosen profession, it is imperative that you take a hard look at your prevailing attitude in each of the primary segments of your life. What is the attitude, what are the feelings behind the attitude, and how can you begin to make attitude adjustments that will change your life for the better?

Relationship Between Emotions and Attitudes

EMOTIONS ---------- THOUGHTS ---------- ATTITUDES

Emotions drive thoughts, which in turn drive attitudes!

Exercise: Attitude Assessment
Since the roots of attitude are anchored in the bucket of emotions that you carry with you (and we each have our bucket), an honest assessment of how you feel about the most important aspects of your life is a good place to start with an attitude assessment.

Step One: With a pen and paper, or notebook, sit down in a quiet place where you will be undisturbed. Go through the list below, one word at a time. Write the word on your paper and say it aloud. ***Quickly capture on paper the first thoughts and feelings that pop into your head***. Do not filter, judge, or question anything; just make the notes about your immediate reactions toward each one.

There are no right answers. This is simply a way to identify the emotions (feelings) that are behind the thoughts that drive your attitudes. Carefully capture every feeling and thought that comes to mind. Honesty is critical. If you lie to yourself, the exercise will be useless.

If you are ready – begin!

YOU
- Your body
- Your looks
- Your style
- Who you are
- Who you want to be

RELATIONSHIPS

Home
Spouse/significant other/roommate
Children
Parents
Siblings
Grandparents
In-laws
Friends

WORK

Your boss
Direct reports
Colleagues
The work itself
The company (or organization)
Your future in the company

COMMUNITY

Your country
The economy
Your church or religious beliefs

LIFE

Being – on this planet, at this time
How your life is right now
How your life will be in the future
Your career
Your hopes and dreams

Step Two: Now, study your notes and think about how your thoughts and feelings are impacting your attitude. What is the prevailing attitude toward each person or situation on the list? Is it positive or negative?

1. What is your attitude about yourself?

2. What is your attitude toward others?
3. What is your attitude about work?
4. What is your attitude about the world around you?
5. What is your attitude about life in general?

Are you positive and generally happy most of the time? Or – are you negative and critical most of the time? Or – is it a mix? If it is a mix, try to identify the dominant attitude in each of the five aspects. Then, taking all the information into account, on which end of the arrow would you place yourself overall? Again – BE HONEST!

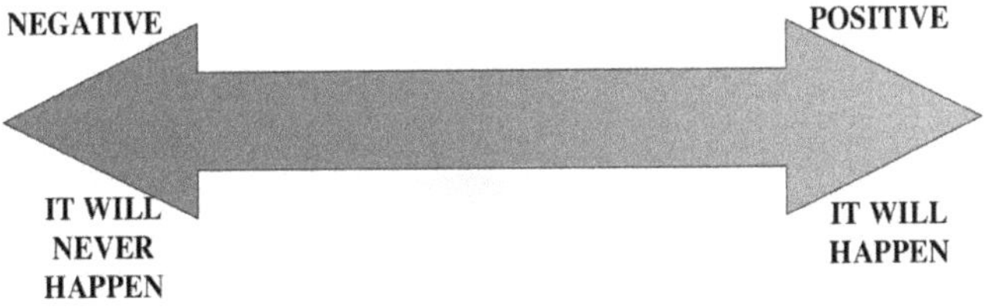

A positive, happy, optimistic attitude is always going to paint your world with much greater joy and sunshine than the attitudes that move closer to the opposite end of the arrow. The optimistic attitude will serve you and support you in everything you do – just as a good friend would; where the pessimistic, negative, angst-filled attitude will tend to defeat you.

Depending on where your attitude is today, it could take some serious work to develop an attitude that will be your friend, rather than your enemy, but it is well worth the time and effort you will put forth.

As you begin to make the adjustments and move toward the positive attitude end of the arrow, your life will begin to change – slowly at first, then more rapidly as you move closer and closer to the positive end of the arrow. You will be in good company because your new best friend, Mr. or Ms. Positive Attitude, will lead the way.

Pay Attention to Your Feelings

There is a great little story that introduces my next point. It may be familiar, but worth repeating in this context.

If you drop a frog in a pan of boiling water, he will jump out immediately to save himself.

On the other hand - If you put a frog in a pan of cold water; set the pan on the stove; and turn the heat on very, very low, the water will heat so gradually that the frog will not notice the change in temperature and will die when the water begins to boil.

This is what happens when you "stuff" your feelings over and over again, year-after-year. You become desensitized to the messages that your emotions are sending you. As a result you refuse to acknowledge and manage the emotions when they surface. You risk dying internally from the heat generated by the constant stuffing and simmering of those emotions.

The biggest challenge will be to have the courage to begin paying attention to your feelings and to identify the emotions that are driving your thoughts and your attitudes. You must look at them carefully and do the work that is necessary to shift them into more positive emotions that will generate more positive thoughts and ultimately lead to a more positive attitudes toward people, places and things.

Everyone has their own personal bag of negative emotions and feelings as a result of past experiences. Everyone, and for our purposes today – **YOU specifically** also have the ability to choose whether the contents of the bag will overwhelm you and control you attitude toward everything in your life – or not!

It is time to leave behind all the emotional debris from the past that you have been carrying around. Some of the debris may have come from a parent's unrelenting cross words spoken in frustration or as a result of worry and exhaustion. Some of it may have come from things others did to you – physical, mental or emotional abuse. Whatever its source – it is in the past; and yet, it is making you feel bad. It is time to leave behind all experiences and related emotions that are not doing you any favors and continue to color your world with gloom and doom.

It is vital that you acknowledge and accept that your negative emotions come from past experiences. The feelings/emotions may have been valid at one time, but they are NOT VALID NOW! You can choose to stay mired in those old feelings and let them control your thoughts, which continually reflect in your attitude, but it is not in your best interest to do so. That choice results in an attitude that is a powerful enemy and will prevent you from realizing the happiness that is available to you.

Before we look at specifics about how to deal with the emotions and how to begin developing a more positive outlook on life, let's explore five common emotions that definitely affect attitude.

Five Common Emotions that Affect Attitude

As a child, others were generally responsible for the anxiety, confusion, and hurt that you experienced. As an adult, **you** are responsible for the pain. When you continually judge yourself; neglect, ignore or stuff your feelings; and make others responsible for your pain or happiness, you are abdicating your power to take care of yourself and create the life you want.

The reality is that as an adult, you must choose to take responsibility for the way you are feeling, the way you think, and the attitudes that you project into the world.

The following five emotions always affect a person's attitude, unless the individual has learned to manage them.

REGRET: Thinking about what might have been, and all the woulda, coulda, shoulda's in your life is a useless practice. Stewing about missed opportunities is a waste of time and energy. This is learned behavior that you picked up at some point in your life – probably from someone in your family or a very close friend. The good news is that you can also let it go. Reviewing a missed opportunity or a questionable decision and learning from it is one thing, but going over it again and again is not only useless, it is harmful to your outlook on life (your attitude).

ANGER: This can be a trigger reaction to any perceived attack – physical or emotional. Anger generates negative energy that when not diffused can explode in an instant and hurt anyone in its path, including innocent bystanders, like children. When it simmers just under the surface all the time, it manifests itself in your attitude and sucks up energy that could be used in much more constructive ways.

When you feel anger starting to boil up inside of you, try to remove yourself from the situation and go through the *exercise* explained below – taking deep breaths as you do it. This will help you diffuse the anger and change your focus to something more positive that will allow you to use your energy for something good. The exercise will help you choose to think and behave differently not only in the current situation, but in all similar situations in the future.

SADNESS: This one is worse than anger because it completely depletes your energy and your will to go on. This one is not so easy to diffuse – especially if it is part of a grieving process. Sadness has to drain away slowly at its own pace – letting time heal. But – be aware that you cannot let it linger! If it persists beyond a reasonable length of time, consciously force it out! Work hard to find things that make you laugh and that help you begin to enjoy life again.

For sadness the *exercise* will be even more critical – focus on things to look forward to and to feel positive about. Continuing to feel deep sadness will not change the reality of the source of your sadness. Remember the feeling was valid in the past, but is NOT VALID NOW. Seek and accept relief and peace of mind as your right.

RESENTMENT: People can get caught in the resentment trap, feeling that life has treated them unfairly – nothing ever works out – everyone else always gets the brass ring, etc. Maybe you have had some experiences that seemed extremely unfair, but ***face it - life is not always fair.*** It is unrealistic to expect it to always be fair. Holding on to resentment is not the way to handle that reality. Get over it and get back into the game. Use the *exercise* to let go of the resentment.

GUILT: Feeling guilty is a complete waste of time and energy. It serves no purpose because it does not change a thing! Everyone makes mistakes that hurt others, but what you did or did not do is water under the bridge. You can be sorry, you can apologize, and you can make amends to the degree possible, *but that is all you can do.*

This is one of the most crippling emotions because it can stop you dead in your tracks and prevent you from moving on to experiences that bring happiness and contentment. And - it colors your attitude about almost everything. Use the *exercise* to let it go and to move on to emotions and activities that will better serve you by helping you develop a more positive attitude about life.

MANAGE YOUR EMOTIONS

You must be willing to look at your feelings and emotions, acknowledge them, recognize that they come from past experiences, and do whatever it takes to diffuse them so they no longer erode your happiness. The following exercise can be a great tool for that purpose.

Exercise: Managing Emotions
It is important to talk aloud through each step.

Recognize that you are feeling an emotion that is not serving you.

Identify it, for example: fear, anxiety, feeling worthless, depression, anger, resentment, frustration, abandonment, sadness, etc.

Acknowledge that the emotion stems from something that happened in the past. (*NOTE: It is not necessary to figure out where the feeling comes from or to remember the exact experiences that are at its root. DO NOT spend time trying to do that, it is not important in this exercise.)*

State that the emotion was valid in the past, but it is NOT valid now.

Choose to NOT entertain the emotion any longer because "... it does not serve me."

Choose to feel differently, "I choose to feel ______ "(*name an emotion if you can).* Then continue by saying, "I look forward to_____ *(name something good in your life to focus on and identify activities that you will enjoy and can look forward to doing.)*

The exercise would go something like this:

I recognize that I am feeling bad right now. I am overwhelmed with sadness.

I know that the feeling comes from my past. Feeling sad was valid then, but it is NOT VALID NOW!

*I **choose** NOT to entertain the sadness any longer because it does not serve me.*

*I **choose instead** to feel happy about ______. (Choose something in your life that makes you feel good and identify activities that you can look forward to doing.)*

Examples:
I choose to feel happy about my beautiful family, and the time that I will spend with my daughter tonight before I put her to bed.

I choose to feel happy about the fun I will have playing with my dog later today.

I choose to think about how nice it will be to sit down to dinner with my family and talk about the day.

I choose to think about how proud I am of my son for being so kind to his little sister this morning when she hurt her hand.

I choose to think about my best friend, Alex, and the fun we are going to have this weekend.

The best approach is to go through the exercise four or five times a day even when nothing is bothering you. Say the steps aloud in generic form just for practice. This helps when you actually face a negative emotion because the words will come more easily and you can really focus on the steps and the power that they have to make you feel better.

As you continue to work with the exercise, you will begin to feel the inner peace and joy that come from knowing that you are choosing to think and behave in ways that support your well-being.

Remember: This must be an on-going effort – today, tomorrow, the day after, and the day after that . . . Don't expect magical, immediate results. Change requires commitment, focus, and persistence. It happens a little bit at a time.

It has taken all your life to get you where you are today – so it will take some time to diffuse the emotions and to change the thoughts that affect your attitude. Change always requires patience and never happens as fast as we want it to – so be patient with yourself.

Even though it takes time, I want to emphasize that changing negative thought patterns that result from emotions tied to past experiences is easier that you think. Your reaction may be, "Well, it probably works for some people, but I can't believe that it will work for me. My life is such a mess and the problems are too deep!"

My response to that is – Yes, it can work for you, if you are willing to do the work.

Have you ever noticed that as soon as a huge 757 Jet is parked at the gate the ground crew quickly places wooden blocks in front and in back of each of the wheels to keep it from moving? It seems impossible that those small wood blocks could prevent that giant plane from rolling, but they do. Obviously, if the jet were powered up, the logs would serve no purpose at all. The plane would quickly and easily roll over them and move toward its destination.

It works the same for humans. You can power up and rapidly move forward past the obstacles that are holding you in place; obstacles that have kept you in "park" for far too long.

Diffusing deep-seated emotions that come from your past and letting them go does not mean that you must forget your past and where you have been. It simply means that where you have been is not the only place to be. Your actions are a way of accepting responsibility for your life and giving notice that where you have been is not where you want to be now.

Part Two

Definition of a Positive Attitude

We have been discussing how to make your attitude your friend – in other words, developing an attitude that will color your world in hues and shades of happiness and contentment.

Below is checklist of common characteristics that would be demonstrated by a person with a positive attitude. Take a moment and identify the ones that apply to you right now – and also select two or three that you would like to begin incorporating into your personality.

- Cheerful and friendly
- Energetic and upbeat
- Always considers the glass half full – not half empty
- Has a genuine concern for the people in his/her life

- Is caring, compassionate, and kind to everyone
- Sees the humor in life
- Knows how to laugh with others and at him or herself – and laughs often
- Has a desire to make other people's lives better and looks for ways to make it happen
- Accepts people for who they are – is never critical
- Never purposefully hurts anyone's feelings
- Avoids the gossip mill and never speaks ill of others
- Rather than complain, he or she actively looks for and finds solutions to problems
- No challenge is too big – believes there is always a way to succeed
- Finds beauty in everything
- Always looks for the good in every person and situation
- Speech patterns are filled with positive words – avoids the negative
- Always has fun, may even seem silly at times
- Does not use sarcasm (believes that it is a form of hurtfulness shrouded in humor)
- Gives willingly of his/her knowledge, time, and energy without expecting anything in return
- Believes that life is filled with possibilities and is open and accepting of opportunities that come his/her way
- Develops solid goals and willingly does the work to achieve them
- Enjoys life and looks forward to each new day

How did you do? Were you completely honest? What would happen if you gave that list to five other people? Would their choices in describing you be the same as yours?

This is the list to use as your benchmark. If you really want to be known as a person with a positive attitude and to enjoy all the benefits that come from that, your goal should be to develop every characteristic on that list. It should describe you perfectly – without any reservations.

Identifying the difference between positive behaviors and negative ones is quite easy. What is not so easy is changing personal habits that are deeply ingrained in your behavior patterns. The attitudes that you project day in and day out have developed slowly, over time and are most likely a significant part of your personality. Changing them will take focus, discipline and daily activities that move you in the right direction. It will require making conscious new choices every day.

Do not make the mistake of trying to do everything at once. Focus your energy one-day-at-a-time. Start with the one or two characteristics that you selected from the list and stay with those for a while. Studies show that it takes at least 16 days to establish a new habit. Once you start feeling comfortable with those one or two characteristics, and they have become natural and habitual, take on a couple more.

Actions that Will Build a Positive Attitude

There are eight specific sets of behaviors that when implemented and sustained will become the foundation for a positive outlook on life. Development of any or all of these behaviors will contribute to your general health, your level of self-confidence, and your general well-being – all of which impact your attitude.

Build and maintain a healthy body! Eat well, exercise regularly, and get plenty of rest (develop the habit of power naps if getting a full night's sleep is a challenge in your home).

It is very hard to be positive when you are hungry, exhausted, have limited physical stamina, or if you do not feel well.

Walk straight and tall - carry yourself with confidence – and smile. It is almost impossible to feel depressed and negative when your shoulders are square, your back is straight and you have a smile on your face.

Watch your body language – Make sure that it is congruent with your words? Do your non-verbal messages match the words that you are saying? Or – are you saying one thing and sending a completely different message through your tone of voice and your body language?

According to Albert Mehrabian's research in 1971, 55% of communication is through body language. His conclusion was that communication, on a face-to-face basis, consists of three separate elements that are not of equal importance.

Words are the least important element when communicating. Below are the percentages of the overall message that is conveyed by each of the three elements.

Words (what is actually said) - 7%
Tone of voice (How it is said) - 38%
Body Language - 55%

Live in the present! Too many present moments pass by without notice. Pay attention to what is happening in the here and now. Avoid living your life in limbo - thinking about what is going on somewhere else, worrying about the past, and constantly looking to the future. When you spend all of your time letting your mind wander elsewhere, the present quickly passes you by and you cannot get it back.

The present is the only time in life that has any true value. It is the only time in which you can take action and make a difference – use each present moment wisely!

Be responsible for your life! *Responsibility means: **the ability to respond*** – the ability to choose your response -

the ability to act, rather than react. You have the power to choose to live your life the way you want to live it.

You cannot control the circumstances or events that happen around you - or to you, but you can control how you respond to them. You can live your life by choice – not by default.

Viktor Frankl, a Holocaust survivor, wrote about his experience in a magnificent little book titled, *Man's Search for Meaning:*

> One day, naked and alone in a small room, I began to become aware of what I later called the last of the human freedoms. They could control my entire environment, they could do what they wanted to my body, but I could decide within myself how all of this was going to affect me. Between what happened to me and my response to it, was my freedom or power to choose that response.

Recognize the power of your word! Keeping your word demonstrates to others the kind of person you are. Don't let false promises, frivolous words, falsehoods, or cutting remarks be part of your behavior. When you say something – you should mean it. Say what you mean and mean what you say. When you promise or commit to do something, do it – no excuses. If you can't do it, don't make the promise. When you agree to be somewhere at a certain time – be there at that time.

Being true to your word builds trust and contributes significantly to your self-esteem – both of which lead to a more positive attitude.

Set challenging goals and follow through on them. Do not overwhelm yourself. Pick one or two that are doable and measurable and make them happen. Be excited about the challenge and celebrate when you succeed. Then, pick a couple more. "Rinse and repeat!"

Create a mental picture of yourself as a person with a magnetic positive attitude. Never permit the picture to fade. Begin and end your day with it in your mind and think about it many times throughout the day. When the picture stays clear and prominent in your thoughts, it has the power to pull you into the future.

Create the picture in words, as well – write the description in your journal, so that it is always accessible, in case it begins to dim for any reason! Carry a copy of the description with you and commit yourself to becoming that person, no matter how long it takes.

Activities to Integrate Positive Characteristics into Attitude

Start your day at home **with** ***"good morning" and a smile for each member of your household.*** (Be prepared, if this is not your usual routine, you may get some resistance or weird looks. Don't let that stop you, just keep doing it.)

End your day by making two entries in a personal journal:

> *List three things that you are grateful for.*
>
> *List three successes of the day.* Keep in mind that successes can be very small accomplishments – anything you do that makes a difference in your life or in the life of someone else counts.

Treat every person you come in contact with as the most important person in your life – because at that moment they should be.

When talking to others, give them your full attention. Don't look around, think about other things, or read/send text messages.

Smile and say hello to people in your office, on the street, and in random places. You may be surprised at how good it feels.

When you run into a grumpy, unpleasant clerk or colleague, respond with sincere kindness and pleasantries. For example, you could say something like, "You seem to be having a bad day, is there anything I could do that would make you feel better?" (This is not always easy, but it can be done, and it is fun when you actually do it.)

Commit to having at least one "negative-free day" each week. On these days, watch your thoughts and words very carefully. When you catch yourself thinking or saying anything negative, critical, or a form of complaining, stop yourself immediately and say, "Erase! Erase!" Follow the "erase" with a conscious verbal replacement of the negatives with positives about the person or situation.

If you find yourself in a group of complainers, politely excuse yourself and "erase" the negative thoughts and words from you mind.

Throughout the day, be as positive as you can in everything that you do. Notice how others react to you. There is nothing better than seeing the results firsthand. Are people friendlier? Do they seem to help you out more than usual?

Notice other things that happen during the day, especially how the positive attitude influences other things in your life.

Find a way to let off steam. Create a place in your mind that is your ideal paradise, it may be something as simple as a quiet comfortable room, or as magnificent as a beach in a far-away place. When you feel stressed or struggling with any negative emotion such as anger, remove yourself from the situation if at all possible and go to your mental paradise. Breathe deeply and let yourself relax. When you have calmed down, run through the exercise a few times, and let go of all the negativity that was threatening to take over.

Manage your stress. A few things are help relieve stress are: learn to meditate; manage your time wisely; learn to say "No"; do not try to be all things to all people; use deep breathing and quick tension-release exercises; keep a journal, etc. Find some methods that work for you, and use them regularly.

Do something you love on a regular basis. Dance, play golf, paint, write, play basketball, swim, run, watch a funny movie, go out to dinner with friends, take your grandchild to the park, etc. Doing something you enjoy that will raise your spirits and allow you to maintain a positive attitude.

Have a cache of happy memories, stories, sayings that make you smile. You can pull from this memory collection when you need to shift your mind to happier thoughts and when you attitude needs a little "perk me up."

Be adventurous! Explore new things. Instead of walking away from the unknown, walk towards it.

Embrace challenges – in fact, seek them out! Let yourself accept challenges and find creative ways to deal with them.

Use your imagination – dare to dream and fantasize! The imagination is a wonderful thing. Allow yourself to go to some make believe place. Briefly escape from your regular life by pretending you are someone else, somewhere else. Have fun and be sure to smile.

Avoid negative external voices. Be aware of the words and ideas that you allow into your mind. Television, radio, newspapers, some movies, books, and even song lyrics are filled with violence and negativity. Try to cut these "voices" out of your life, or at least limit them. This also includes friends and family members who are trapped in their own negative dialogs. Keep your exposure to negativity to a minimum.

Be selective in the people that you choose to hang out with. When you spend time with positive people, their attitudes tend to rub off on you – and the same is true when you spend time with negative people. So, be careful and choose wisely.

You may even want to consider starting an informal optimist club where a group agrees to support one another in their efforts to develop more positive attitudes.

You can take these suggestions and build upon them. Include other activities that make you happy. You know better than anyone what makes you smile, so take these suggestions as a starting point and run with it. Let your new best friend, Mr. or Ms. Positive Attitude guide you.

CONCLUSION

As you begin to think, speak and act more positively, the negatives will begin to fade into the background. It may seem that everything around you is changing, when in reality it is you that is changing. In all likelihood you will begin to notice little things that make you smile – things that you would have flown right by you in the past.

If you stick with the process, momentum will build and your attitude will improve day-by-day, creating a whole new outlook on life. You will be using all your energy in positive pursuits and the negative energy that was previously holding you back will disappear from your life.

Please keep in mind that a positive attitude does not mean that your life will be perfect, that good things will always happen to you and that you will never have problems. This is life we are talking about, and we all know there are no guarantees.

What it does ensure, however, is that developing a positive attitude will help you face problems and challenges without getting angry, upset, or depressed. Adversity will no longer frighten or overwhelm you because you will grow to realize that are always solutions to problems and effective ways to handle difficult situations.

Essentially, you will have the ability to respond to anything that life throws at you in a way that makes everything manageable and ultimately OK.

As was explained at the beginning of the book, a positive attitude is a powerful thing. It will start to shape your view of everyone and everything around you and impact others in very positive ways. You will see its incredible influence almost immediately.

We have come full circle in our discussion, now it is up to you

Ask yourself: How do I want to live my life? What will be the hues and shades in the picture that I paint with my attitude? Am I willing to do the work that will help me make the necessary attitude adjustments so that my whole outlook on life is brand new?

Keep in mind that your emotions, thoughts and actions create your attitude. The happier you are, the better your attitude will be. The better your attitude is, the happier you will be. It is a wonderful self-perpetuating cycle!

Enjoy the new world that awaits you!

Nancy N. Wilson

P. S. There is a wonderful book by John Kabat-Zinn that I highly recommend. It dovetails beautifully with the information I have shared with you. I promise it is worth reading: *Mindfulness for the Beginner.*

REFERENCES

Amos, J. A. (18 December 2010). *Body Language to Convey Status, Hierarchy or Dominance.* Retrieved August 30, 2012 from: http://www.bodylanguageexpert.co.uk/BodyLanguageAndStatusHierarchyDominance.html

Freeman, A. & DeWolf, R. (1990 – Harper Perennial Edition). *Woulda/Coulda/Shoulda – Overcoming Regrets, Mistakes, and Missed Opportunities.* Harper Collins Publishers. New York, NY 10022.

Schiraldi, G. R. (2007). *10 Simple Solutions for Building Self-Esteem - How to End Self-Doubt, Gain Confidence & Create a Positive Self-Image.* New Harbinger Publications, Inc. Oakland, CA 94609.

Williams, H. Jr. (1985). *Attitude Adjustment* (Lyrics by Hank Williams, Jr.) Retrieved August 30, 2012 from: http://www.uulyrics.com/music/hank-williams-jr/song-attitude-adjustment/

"It was an attitude adjustment
It made my whole outlook brand new
Just an attitude adjustment
It made my whole outlook brand new"

About the Author

Nancy N Wilson, an Arizona native, has enjoyed tremendous opportunities both personally and professionally. She has lived and worked on both the East Coast and West Coast of the United States. She had a long career as a management consultant for major corporations in the U.S., with accounts in Europe and Japan. Her area of expertise was management and leadership development. She has also traveled extensively throughout Central and South America.

In 2007, she returned to Arizona to live nearer her two sons and to do what she has always wanted to do – WRITE. Her primary goal was to become a published author. She has now realized that dream and hopes to be writing and publishing for many years to come.

In addition to this book, she has also authored *Candy Making Made Easy, Instructions & 16 Starter Recipes,* and the highly successful *Mama's Legacy Cookbook Series,* which includes seven volumes.

All of her books are listed on the following page. They can be purchased through Amazon.com at The Kindle Store.

Get your copies today!

Other Books by This Author

Candy Making Made Easy
Instructions and 17 Starter Recipes

Cake Making Made Easy
Instructions and 60 Cakes
Plus Frosting, Icing, Glaze and Filling Recipes

Mama's Legacy Cookbook Series

Seven Volumes Available

Dinner – 27 Easy Recipes (Volume I)

Breakfast and Brunch – 31 Delicious Recipes **(Volume II)**

Dessert – 31 Scrumptious Recipes **(Volume III)**

Chicken – 25 Classic Recipes (**Volume IV)**

Mexican Favorites – 21 Traditional Recipes **(Volume V)**

Side Dishes – 41 Great Recipes **(Volume VI)**

Sauce Recipes – 50 Tasty Choices **(Volume VII)**

CPSIA information can be obtained
at www.ICGtesting.com
Printed in the USA
BVHW040953191218
535962BV00016B/2736/P

9 781479 326136